THE A-Z
OF
HOMEMADE
SYRUPS
& CORDIALS

Words by Amelia Carruthers
Illustrations and Design by Zoë Horn Haywood

CONTENTS

Introduction 1

Equipment and Preparation 3

Recipes 5

    A is for. . . Aniseed 6

    B is for. . . Blackberry 8

    C is for. . . Cherry 10

    D is for. . . Dandelion 12

    E is for. . . Elderflower 14

    F is for. . . Filtering 17

    G is for. . . Ginger 18

    H is for. . . History! 20

    I is for. . . Ingredients 22

    J is for. . . . Juniper 24

    K is for. . . Kiwi 26

    L is for. . . Lavender 28

    M is for. . . Mango 30

    N is for. . . Nectarine 32

    O is for. . . . Orange 34

CONTENTS

P is for. . . Pineapple 36

Q is for. . . Quince 38

R is for. . . Raspberry 40

S is for. . . Strawberry.. 42

T is for. . . The Tropics! 44

U is for. . . Uses 47

V is for. . . Vessels 48

W is for. . . Whitecurrants 50

X is for. . . Xmas 52

Y is for. . . Yuletide.. 54

Z is for. . . Zest 56

Ten Top Tips and Tricks.. 58

INTRODUCTION

It is incredibly easy to make syrups and cordials at home. Essentially the process involves steeping or cooking your chosen ingredients in liquids – waiting – straining – and then consuming! Cordials are the historical descendants of herbal medicines; they were made in Italy as early as the thirteenth century and were often prepared by monks and other healers. Nowadays, syrups and cordials are made worldwide and served in many ways: by themselves, poured over ice or ice-cream, with cocktails or with any manner of dessert. Some are prepared by infusing certain woods, fruits or flowers in water, and adding sugar or other items, and yet others are distilled from aromatics.

To make a syrup or cordial, the preliminary ingredients are usually cooked, be it spices, vanilla, flowers, caramel, peppermint, fruits, coffee...etc. with a basic syrup, consisting of roughly equal amounts of sugar and water. The mix is then brought to the boil, simmered for a further twelve to twenty minutes and taken off the heat. It is then strained if necessary. This rough guide will of course change from recipe to recipe, though it is a good place to start. The wonderful thing about making your own homemade products is the fun one can have with creating customised labels and garnishes to the finished bottles (think berries, citrus zest, herb sprigs) – a perfect present as well as personal treat. We hope that the reader is inspired by this book to start making their own syrups and cordials, a delicious as well as rewarding pastime. Enjoy.

Amelia Carruthers

EQUIPMENT AND PREPARATION

The equipment needed for cordial and syrup making is rather basic, and you may already have most of it around the house. You will need saucepans, any earthenware or non-porous bowls and either glass or plastic bottles (size and amount dependent on the batch size you are intending), as well as material (usually muslin) for straining. When you have cooked the ingredients in a saucepan (heavy bottomed jam boilers work best), you may find it useful to purchase a stand or tripod, from which to leave the mixture to strain overnight. This is by no means necessary though, and a sieve and wooden spoon would work just as well for smaller batches! Although the types of saucepans, bowls and bottles you will need to make cordials with are not difficult to find, it is important that you take the time to get your equipment ready before you start making your first batch.

Always ensure the fruits that you use in your syrup or cordial recipes have been washed thoroughly, especially if they have been gathered from low hedgerows, or bushes that are near roads. If the fruits have pips or cores, you may wish to remove these before cooking, as some may leave a bitter taste to the final product. Some however, such as rosehips are perfectly fine to add whole; just remember to strain thoroughly before the final stages...

All the recipes in this book will use roughly 500g of fruit

(if this is the main ingredient), which should produce roughly 700ml of syrup / cordial. The amount of syrup and cordial you produce will depend on how strong you wish the end result to be. Some people prefer much thicker, viscous syrups, whilst others will only be looking for a lightly flavoured cordial. Other ingredients such as lavender, cinnamon, aniseed or ginger will require less 'primary ingredient' though, as their natural flavours are so strong. Have fun experimenting and just use what you've got!

RECIPES

A IS FOR... ANISEED

The distinctive taste of aniseed, from the anise flower, is the perfect ingredient to use in a cordial. You will only need a little, as the aniseed flavour really comes through in this drink. Diluted with a little water, this makes a wonderful alcohol-free aperitif, much like the traditional French beverage, Pastis. Enjoy as a refreshing mid-day drink, or as a before-dinner palate cleanser!

Aniseed Cordial

Ingredients

- 30g Aniseed
- 225g Sugar
- 1 litre of Water

Method

1. This is such a simple recipe to make: In a heavy-bottomed saucepan, gently heat all the ingredients until the sugar has dissolved. This should take about ten minutes.
2. Strain the liquid through a clean muslin cloth.
3. Pour into sterilised bottles to store – and keep in the fridge or freezer.

B IS FOR...
BLACKBERRY

When making cordials and syrups the soft fruits are a great place to start. Blackberries are wonderful little fruits, found all over England, most often growing wild in hedgerows. During the autumn months when they are in abundance, why not gather some up to make this delicious fruit cordial. Make sure you rinse the fruit thoroughly before you get started.

You could also try using *Blackcurrants* - just add a little more sugar to these small, slightly tart berries. And why not experiment with *Blood Orange Syrup?* - Mixed with sparkling water or wine, it is a delightful pick-me-up for a hot summers day.

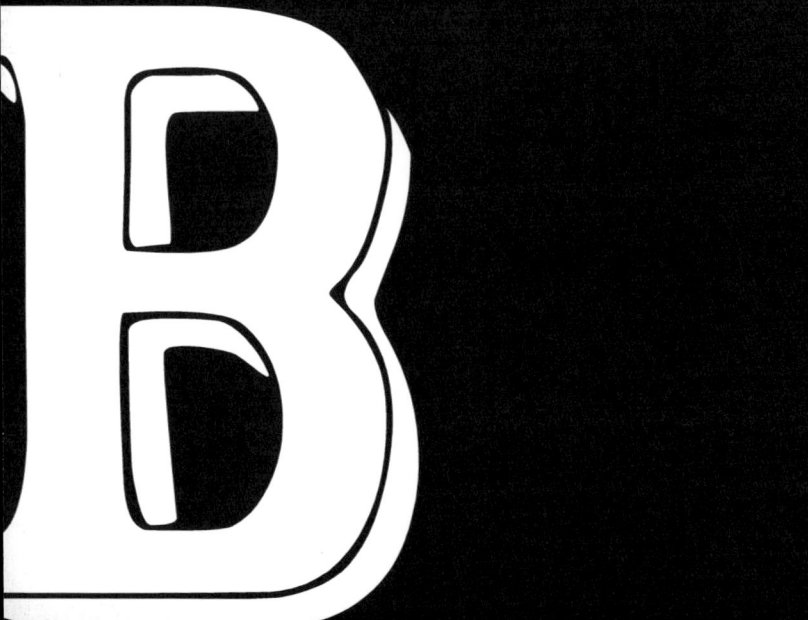

Blackberry Cordial

Ingredients

- 500g Blackberries
- Cold Water (to cover)
- 150g Caster Sugar
- 1 Cinnamon stick
- 1 Lemon

Method

1. Take your (washed) berries and place them in a large saucepan.
2. Pour over the boiling water and cook until the berries start to release their juice. You can mash the berries to aid this juice extraction.
3. Strain off the berries through a clean muslin cloth.
4. Add the sugar, lemon juice and cinnamon (again, to taste) and boil for around fifteen minutes (or until the sugar has completely dissolved), skimming off any scum.
5. Carefully bottle the cordial, seal and store in the fridge.

C IS FOR. . . CHERRY

Cherries and syrups are a match made in heaven! The sweet flavour and vibrant colour of these little stone fruits make them the perfect fruit to use as a base in a syrup. The juice of cherries is wonderfully sweet and slightly syrupy in consistency, lending itself perfectly to this recipe. Cherries are in season during July in the UK, so this is a great recipe to try in the summer. Try adding the syrup to champagne, for a perfect cherry bellini.

Cherry Syrup

Ingredients

- 500g Cherries
- 100g Sugar
- 10g Cornflour
- 1 Cinnamon stick
- A dash of Water

Method

1. Put the cornflour, water and sugar in a pan – cooking at a low heat until it forms a runny paste.
2. Add the cherries and the cinnamon to the pan, adding a little more water if required.
3. Cook the cherries for about twenty minutes.
4. It is (as usual) up to you, whether you strain the cherry fruits at this point, or keep them in the syrup.
5. Allow the mixture to cool, then carefully pour into sterilised bottles or jars.

D IS FOR...
DANDELION

Dandelions are very good for the body, and rather easy to make into a delicious cordial. One of the main benefits of dandelions is that they are very good for the liver. The antioxidants like vitamin-C and Luteolin can keep the liver functioning in optimal gear and protect it from aging. This is also a great cordial to make, as Dandelions appear in almost every garden around Britain, allowing for a bit of home-foraging! Try this subtly flavoured cordial diluted with a little water.

Dandelion Cordial

Ingredients
- 100g (or slightly more) Dandelion Heads
- 650ml Water
- 450g Sugar
- 2 Oranges
- 2 Lemons
- A handful of Raisins

Method

1. Place the dandelions in a large bowl and cover with the boiling water.
2. Allow this mixture to stand for three days, then filter through a clean muslin cloth.
3. Place the liquid in a sterilised bottle with the dissolved sugar, and strained juice of the lemons and oranges.
4. Allow this mixture to stand for at least three days.
5. Decant into smaller bottles to store and (if you like), place two raisins in each bottle before sealing. This will impart a rounder, sweeter flavour.

E IS FOR...
ELDERFLOWER

Elderflowers are the pretty white flowers of the elder tree. They have been used to make beverages for centuries, appearing in abundance in the British hedgerows - and are believed to have a number of health benefits. One of the main health benefits of elderflowers are that they are antioxidants, cleansing the lymph glands and reducing susceptibility to many chronic (mostly age-related) conditions. Elderflowers are best gathered on a warm day (never when wet), just as the many tiny buds are beginning to open. Do remember to leave some flowers for elderberry picking later in the year though! This recipe for elderflower cordial is sweet yet subtly flavoured, and has a gentle, floral aroma. If you are looking for some other flower-based cordial recipes, why not use the same method with Hibiscus flowers? They have a tart, cranberry-like flavour.

Elderflower Cordial

Ingredients

- About 25 Elderflower Heads
- 3 Lemons
- 1 Orange
- 1kg sugar
- 1 heaped tsp. citric acid (optional)
- 1.5 litres of Water

Method

1. Carefully inspect the elderflower heads, making sure to remove any insects. Place them in a large bowl.
2. Zest and juice the lemons and orange, and put this in the bowl with the elderflower. Add the sugar and the citric acid too.
3. Bring 1.5 litres of water to the boil, and pour it over the flowers and zest. Stir.
4. Cover overnight and leave to infuse. It is up to you how long you leave the mixture for – some only do this for a day, others for a week. The longer you leave it, the better the flavour, just make sure to stir it each day. Don't go much over a week though.
5. Strain the liquid through a piece of muslin.
6. Using a funnel, pour the liquid into sterilised bottles. Your cordial is ready to serve!

F IS FOR... FILTERING

Filtering is an easy but essential technique to master, and can be done in a number of ways.

Pouring your cordial or syrup through a clean muslin cloth, or a funnel lined with coffee filter paper to remove any sediment is a simple process which will really add to the quality of your finished beverage. Here, try to avoid (if possible) actively pushing the mixture through the cloth or paper; as this will result in a slightly cloudier end result.

Depending on how much syrup or cordial you have made, filtering may be a two person job! If you only have a little liquid, pouring it through a lined funnel will suffice. However if you have doubled or even tripled our recipies, asking a friend to help you keep the muslin taught over a large bowl or bucket will be an invaluable help! For the more dedicated syrup and cordial maker, you may also consider buying a tripod, from which to hang the filtering material. On your own or with a friend, it's important to get this right.

Some recipes may call for you to filter the liquid a number of times and some may not need filtering at all. Recipes differ greatly, so make sure you read the method instructions carefully before starting work on your first batch.

G IS FOR... GINGER

The warm and spicy flavour of fresh ginger makes a wonderful syrup, and is a very versatile ingredient to have stocked in your drinks cupboard. Try this simple recipe for ginger syrup, which once made, can be added to an array of drinks and cocktails to really spice them up. Unlike most of the other recipes, you will not need that much ginger here, as the flavour is naturally very strong. Added to hot water and lemon, a little ginger syrup is a great natural remedy for sore throats and colds.

Ginger Syrup

Ingredients

- 250g Bruised Ginger
- 1 Lemon
- 750g Sugar
- 1.5 litres of Water

Method

1. Cook the ginger and the water in a saucepan, gently simmering for about half an hour.
2. Add the lemon juice and the sugar and cook for a further fifteen minutes until the sugar has completely dissolved.
3. Strain the liquid through a muslin cloth and pour into sterilised bottles.
4. Seal the bottles and store in the fridge or freezer, ready for use.

H IS FOR... HISTORY!

Cordials and syrups were originally enjoyed in Renaissance Italy. In this period of great cultural change and achievement, which lasted from the fourteenth to the sixteenth century, they were used as tonics and early medicines.

A 'cordial' in its truest sense is any invigorating and stimulating preparation, intended for medicinal purposes. Many early cordials were believed to be especially beneficial to the heart (*cor* in Latin). Many were also considered aphrodisiacs, a view which encouraged their consumption in a social as opposed to a medical context. Other early varieties of alcoholic cordials were flavoured with spices and herbal ingredients, thought to settle the stomach after excessive eating. Popular mixtures included *Rosa Solis*, made in Turin from the sundew plant – thought to invigorate the heart. *Royal Usquebaugh* is an example of a cordial thought to aid digestion, containing flecks of gold leaf, aniseed, liquorice and saffron, sweetened with fruit sugar of figs and raisins. Not one for everyday drinking!

Most syrups and cordials appeared independently. Although first produced in Italian apothecaries during the Renaissance (where they had refined the art of distilling), they were very soon after found in France, referred to as *Liqueurs d'Italie*. This is also where we get the term 'liqueur' from. The first cordials and syrups arrived in England as late as the fifteenth century, and were called 'distilled cordial waters.' These were generally alcoholic medicines, prescribed in small doses to invigorate the heart, body and spirit. It was only in the eighteenth century that people across Europe started making cordials and syrups for recreational consumption. Nowadays, cordials and syrups are especially popular in Western Europe, with many homemade as well as shop-bought varieties, but less so in countries such as America.

I IS FOR...
INGREDIENTS

Making your own cordials and syrups is a fantastic way to use up surplus produce, much of which you may have grown yourself, or naturally foraged. As already noted, the ingredients for syrups and cordials are relatively straightforward.

All the recipes will use sugar and water (to make a basic syrup), but after this - the choice is yours! As a rule, use seasonal fruits as inspiration for your syrup or cordial recipes. This way, your cordials and syrups will be cheap to produce and delicious, as well as lessening your ecological impact. Work out when fruits are in abundance, what time of year is best to pick them, and most importantly, *where* you can find them. In June, elderflowers are just coming out, whilst in July the blackcurrants make an appearance, followed by plums in September. For the more exotic cordial or syrup though, as well as for necessary ingredients such as lemons, your local food-store should have everything you need.

An important question to bear in mind when choosing your ingredients, is - does it have enough flavour when cooked to bear being diluted? Mellow fruits like apples for example, make a wonderfully fresh juice, but once you boil them - adding sugar and water, this will just be a tasteless sugary drink. Crab Apples, Quince and Rosehips have similar, 'earthy' flavours, and make good alternatives to the standard apple. As a rule of thumb, if you could happily eat large quantities of the fruit or other 'main ingredient' in question, then it will probably not make a very good finished cordial.

J IS FOR. . . . JUNIPER

Juniper berries are the base ingredients in gin, giving the spirit its distinctive taste and aroma. As an interesting aside; the juniper berry is not in actual fact a true berry; rather it is a cone with unusually fleshy and merged scales, which give it a berry-like appearance. This recipe for juniper cordial is wonderfully simple to make at home, and has the added accent of coriander, too. You will notice it contains less fruit than most of the other recipes; this is because of the wonderful, strong flavour that juniper's possess. Try mixing it with tonic water and a squeeze of lime for a delicious alcohol-free gin and tonic...

Juniper Cordial

Ingredients

- 15g dried Juniper Berries
- 225ml Water
- One bunch of Coriander
- 225ml Sugar Syrup

Method

1. Crush the juniper berries in a large (sterilised) jar, and add the water.
2. Add the coriander and sugar syrup and shake well.
3. Allow the mixture to stand for two weeks then carefully strain the liquid through a clean muslin cloth.
4. Pour into sterilised bottles to store.

K IS FOR... KIWI

The kiwifruit has an incredibly interesting history. Initially known as the 'Chinese Gooseberry' (the fruit originated in Northern China) it is the edible berry of a woody vine. Cultivation of this fuzzy kiwifruit spread from China in the early twentieth century to New Zealand, where the first commercial plantings occurred. Here, the fruit was called 'yang tao' but was changed to 'Chinese Gooseberry' by the New Zealanders. It proved popular with American servicemen in New Zealand during World War II and after this, the fruit grew in worldwide popularity. Kiwis are naturally a little sour and have a beautiful, bright green colour. This unusual cordial will be sure to impress any visitors, and goes perfectly with lime.

Kiwi Cordial

Ingredients

- 7 Kiwis (cut-up)
- 1 Lime (zested)
- 200g Sugar (more or less according to taste)
- Water to cover

Method

1. Peel and chop the kiwis.
2. Place the kiwis, water, sugar, a little lime juice and zest into a saucepan on a low heat.
3. Cook the mixture until the kiwis are releasing their juices. You may wish to press them against the side of the pan with a fork - to extract the maximum flavour.
4. Let the mixture cool and then strain through a muslin cloth.
5. Decant into sterilised bottles - and your cordial is ready to serve!

L IS FOR... LAVENDER

This recipe uses lavender blossoms – a truly fragrant and delicious way to enhance your syrups! This little purple herb is ideal for adding an aromatic, light botanical flavour to any drink and makes you think immediately of spring. When choosing your lavender use buds that have not opened and flowered completely - for the best aromatic qualities go for the buds that are fully purple but still tightly wrapped. They are highly decorative as well as edible, so why not try adorning your syrup bottle with a sprig of lavender to finish. You can also replace half the sugar with honey, which gives a much rounder finish to the syrup. This syrup is wonderful diluted and enjoyed as a drink, but can also be used to accompany many desserts.

Lavender Flower Syrup

Ingredients

- 100g Lavender Flowers
- 500ml Boiling Water
- 400g Sugar (or partly replace with 200g honey)

Method

1. Place the flowers into a large jar or bowl and pour the boiling water over them.
2. Cover with a clean cloth and leave to stand until cool.
3. Pour the mixture into a heavy-bottomed saucepan with the sugar / honey and boil for ten minutes.
4. Strain the mixture through a clean muslin cloth and pour into sterilised bottles to store.

M IS FOR. . . MANGO

In a very similar manner to cherries, mangoes are another fruit which lend themselves perfectly to cordials and syrups. Mangoes have a lovely, bright orange colour and (like pineapple) a sweet, syrupy juice. This recipe for mango cordial can be diluted and enjoyed as a long drink, with still or sparkling water. As ever, it could also be poured over deserts for a truly tropical flavour!

If you are feeling suitably exploratory, why not try adding some other flavouring to the basic Mango Cordial – ginger and lemongrass are particularly good.

Mango Cordial

Ingredients

- 3 Ripe Mangoes
- 150g Caster Sugar
- Water (to cover)
- For extra (optional) taste:
- 2 Stalks Lemon Grass
- 5cm Piece of Ginger
- 1 Vanilla Pod
- 1 Lime

Method

1. Cook the Mango, sugar (to taste) and water in a large saucepan and heat the fruit until its juices are running freely.

2. At this point, you may want to add extra flavours, in the form of lemon grass, ginger, vanilla and lime juice. Cook the syrup for a further ten minutes to ensure all these flavours are combined.

3. Carefully strain the liquid through a clean muslin cloth.

4. Pour into sterilised jars or bottles to serve.

N IS FOR... NECTARINE

Nectarines are delicious stone fruits, similar to peaches but with a lovely smooth skin. Make sure to buy them when they are in season (and therefore cheaper) - making nectarine syrup is the perfect way to preserve the juices of these fruits to enjoy at a later date. They are naturally sweet and would therefore be delicious with any manner of desserts. The combination of nectarine *and* plum is a fantastic one too, so why not try replacing half the nectarines with plums, for a truly exciting cordial?

Nectarine Syrup

Ingredients

- 500g Nectarines
  (or go half and half with the plums!)
- 150g Sugar (to taste)
- Water (to cover)

Method

1. Fill a sterilised jar 2/3 full with ripe nectarines including the stones. Stand the jar in a saucepan of boiling water and simmer until the fruit is soft and the juice flows freely.

2. Strain the liquid through a clean muslin cloth.

3. Combine the juice and the sugar in a saucepan– (making sure to taste when adding the sugar).

4. Boil the mixture for approximately fifteen minutes, skimming any scum.

5. Allow to cool, and pour into sterilised bottles before storing.

6. Serve as a drink, with sparkling water – or serve as a dessert over waffles, ice-cream, cakes – or any other combination.

O IS FOR. . . . ORANGE

Orange juice is perhaps one of the nation's best loved beverages. For a slightly more unusual take on this classic, combine the juice with zest and sugar, and transform it into a delicious syrup. Try this simple and straightforward recipe for a 'Blood Orange Citrus Sparkler' a modern take on a traditional classic; making a refreshing long beverage. It is best served with sparkling water (or sparkling wine, dependant on preference). This drink is simple and thirst-quenching, as well as taking no time at all to prepare. It is also easy to make in large batches and thus makes the perfect summer daytime tipple.

You could also try this recipe with pink grapefruits, which would be lovely as a sparkling beverage. Do make sure to add more sugar if using grapefruit however, as they can be exceedingly tart!

Blood Orange Syrup

Ingredients

- 150ml of Blood Orange Juice / Pink Grapefruit Juice
- 100g Sugar (more if using Grapefruits)
- A teaspoon of Orange Zest

Method

1. Add the juice and sugar to a saucepan, and cook until the sugar has completely dissolved.
2. Now take it off the heat, add the zest from the oranges, and allow to cool.
3. Strain through a clean piece of muslin, and then decant into sterilised jars or bottles.
4. Your *Citrus Sparkler* is ready to serve!

P IS FOR... PINEAPPLE

This recipe for pineapple syrup makes a wonderfully sweet and sticky juice which is perfect to stock in your kitchen for the summer months. It will give a tropical flair to any dish – sweet or savoury. Mixed with other cordials, or simply sparkling water this is the perfect summer tipple.

Pineapple Syrup

Ingredients

- 500g peeled, sliced Pineapple
- 100ml Water
- 100g Sugar

Method

1. Crush the fruit in a large jar and pour the water over it.
2. Stand the jar in a pan of boiling water and cook gently for two hours until the fruit is tender.
3. Strain the liquid through a clean muslin cloth, and add the sugar to taste.
4. Put the mixture into a saucepan, bring to the boil again and cook for a further fifteen minutes, skimming any scum.
5. Allow to cool, then carefully pour into sterilised bottles to store.

Q IS FOR... QUINCE

Quince are small fruits which belong to the same family as pears - and a much under-used and under-appreciated British fruit. Quince trees are often grown for their pretty pink flowers, but the fruits can be used in jams and preserves, as well as this simple and straightforward recipe for quince syrup. Quince has an earthy flavour, almost a cross between an apple and a pear, and is commonly used as an accompaniment to cheese. Try this syrup as an after dinner aperitif!

Quince Syrup

Ingredients

- 500g fresh, ripe Quinces
- 200g Sugar
- Dash of Water
- 1 Lemon

Method

1. Put the (cut up) quinces, sugar and water in a saucepan, and bring to the boil.
2. Reduce the heat and place a slightly smaller lid over the fruit to keep it submerged.
3. Simmer until the liquid is pale pink and has been reduced to a thin syrup. This will usually take about an hour.
4. Strain the mixture through a clean cloth, and reserve the cooked quines to make some delicious stuffing with.
5. Stir in the lemon juice.
6. Your syrup is ready to serve.

R IS FOR...
RASPBERRY

The brightly coloured juice that you can gather from ripe, fresh raspberries will make this syrup taste as vibrant as it looks. Here is a slightly more complicated Raspberry recipe for a truly delicious syrup. This recipe will be a perfect match to chocolate (especially dark chocolate) desserts, so you may want to make the end-product a bit thicker than usual. The cornflour will help with this, but is entirely optional. Also, feel free to add a little more sugar to this recipe if you raspberries are not at their peak ripeness. You may serve the syrup straight away (warm, over pancakes or ice-cream is a treat), or freeze it to save for later.

Raspberry Syrup

Ingredients

- 500g Raspberries (fresh or frozen)
- 10g Cornflour
- 100g Sugar
- 10g Butter
- A dash of Water
- 1 Lemon (to taste)
- 1 Vanilla Pod (to taste)

Method

1. Add the water, cornflour, lemon and sugar together in a saucepan – heat and stir until it forms a smooth, runny paste.
2. Add the raspberries and cook on a low heat until they begin to break down.
3. It is up to you whether you strain the mixture at this point – to create a smooth syrup. You can alternatively keep the raspberry bits in, for a more full-bodied result.
4. Take the mixture off the heat, and melt in the butter and the vanilla.
5. Decant into bottles and jars, and your raspberry syrup is ready to serve.

S IS FOR...
STRAWBERRY

Here is a really simple recipe for a sweet and vibrant-coloured syrup. The strawberries have a lot of natural sweetness, so do adjust the sugar levels according to your own preferences.
Like the raspberry syrup, strawberry syrup is the perfect addition to desserts, as well as being a really quick and easy way to make a cheats Strawberry Daiquiri...

Strawberry Syrup

Ingredients

- 500g Strawberries
- 150g Sugar (to taste, depending on tartness of strawberries)
- 200ml Cold Water

Method

1. Place the strawberries, sugar and water in a heavy-bottomed saucepan and heat gently until the juices flow freely.
2. Strain the juice through a clean muslin cloth.
3. Heat the mixture for a further five minutes, skimming any scum which rises to the top.
4. Allow the mixture to cool slightly, and pour into sterilised bottles before storing.

T IS FOR...
THE TROPICS!

This recipe for a tropical passionfruit syrup makes a rich and sweet liquid, perfect for storing in your cupboard for the hot summer months. Also known as 'grenadilla', passion fruit is a tropical fruit about the size of an egg with a brittle outer shell that contains crunchy seeds surrounded by intensely flavoured, slightly sour, yellow, juicy pulp. Its inedible shell can either be purple or yellow in colour, so don't worry which ones you get. Try this syrup with a dash of lime, mint and the actual passionfruit seeds for a fun and exotic cocktail (with or without alcohol). Top up with anything sparkling!

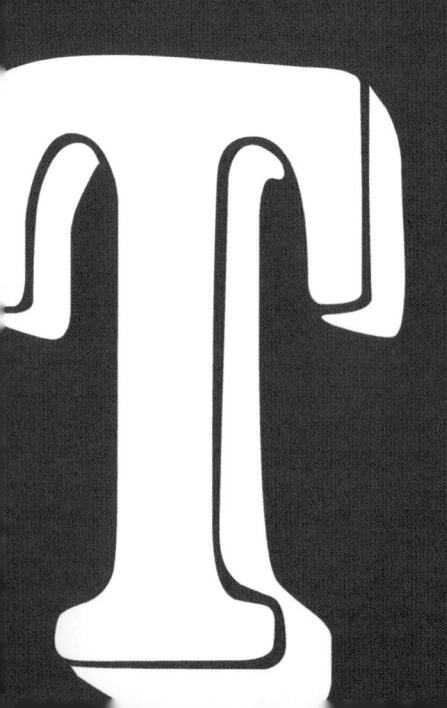

Passionfruit Syrup

Ingredients

- 250ml Passionfruit Pulp
- 225g Sugar
- 1 Lemon
- Ice cubes and sparkling water, to serve (optional)

Method

1. Place the sugar, water and juice (zest if you want too) in a saucepan over a low heat.
2. Cook until the sugar dissolves, then bring to the boil.
3. Simmer for five minutes, or until the syrup thickens slightly. At this point, stir in the passionfruit pulp.
4. Set aside to cool.
5. Strain the syrup through a fine sieve, pushing the pulp through with the back of a spoon if necessary. This should be a reasonably thick syrup.
6. Pour your liquid into an airtight bottle and seal - it is ready to serve!

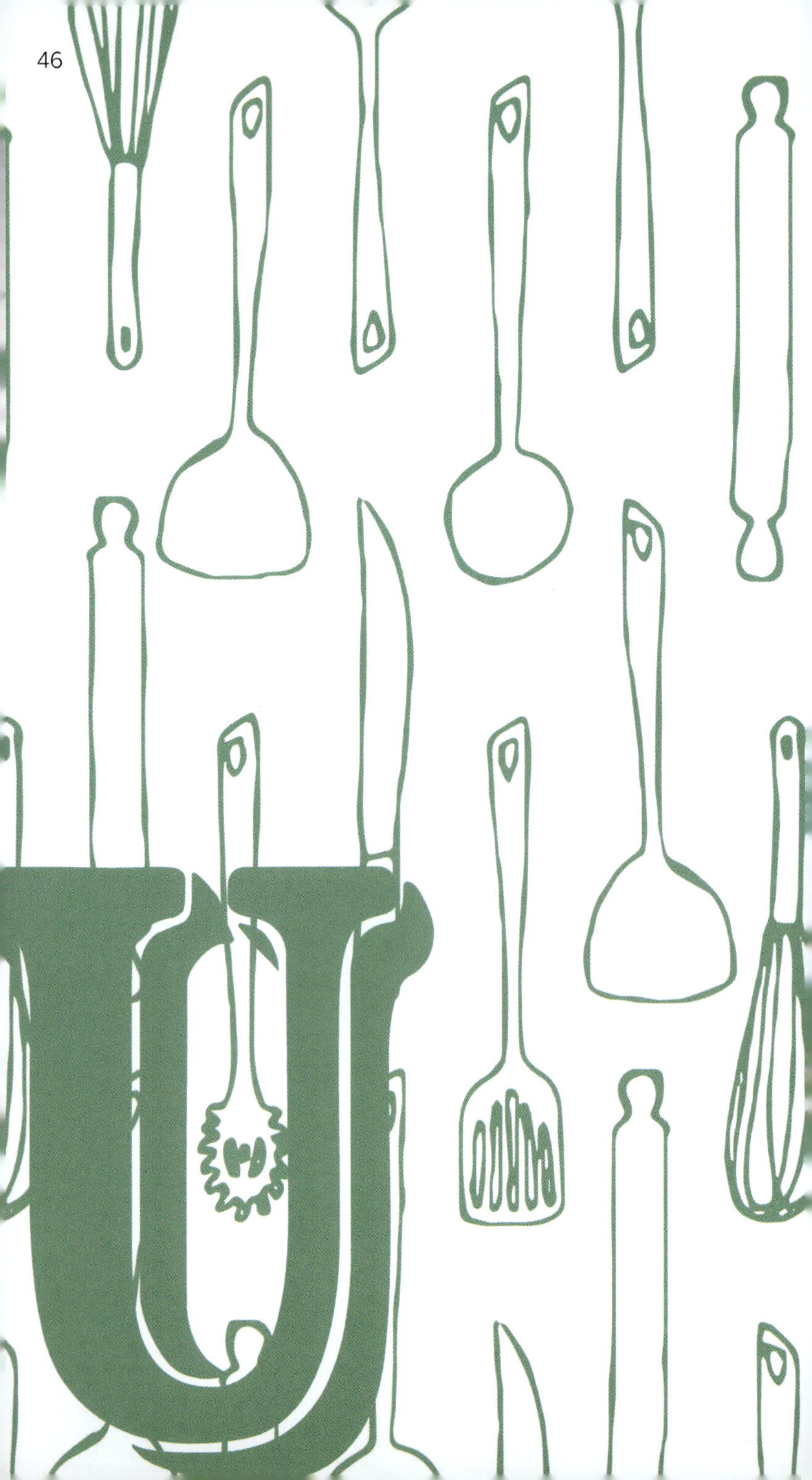
U

U IS FOR... USES

Syrups and cordials are incredibly handy staples to have stored in your fridge. They have many uses and can be rather versatile. Try adding them to cocktails to really enhance the flavour, or experiment with homemade syrups as additions or garnishes to desserts. The vibrant colour and bold flavours will really add to a fruity pudding, and any berry syrups are fantastic paired with chocolate. For something a bit more unusual, try the fragrant lavender syrup with ice cream or a creme brulee. It also goes wonderfully with honey.

In terms of non-alcoholic drinks, serve your homemade cordials with a splash of water (sparkling water adds a nice touch), diluting them to your preferred strength. Mixed with fruit and lemonade, they would be a great addition to any party. A jug filled with plenty of ice is a nice way to mix your cordials, and you can add some sprigs of herbs (rosemary or mint are particularly nice), flowers or slices of fruit / peeled zest to really add to the flavour. For a twist on the classic gin and tonic (with or without the gin!), try a slice of cucumber with the juniper cordial.

V IS FOR... VESSELS

Using the correct vessel when making cordials and syrups at home is very important. Glass jars for preparation and large bottles for storage work best. The best kind of bottle to use is a large glass Demijohn (although this is by no means the only option – standard plastic bottles work better if you are wishing to freeze the liquid). Experiment with smaller bottles to store your syrups and cordials too - this way they will make lovely gifts for your friends. Whatever vessels you choose, they must be collectively large enough to hold all of your liquid, and must also be sealable.

When actually making your syrups and cordials, sourcing some large glass jars will be helpful. Some of the recipes work best when the fruit is cooked in these sealed containers (as opposed to directly in the saucepan) - as it preserves more of the delicious juices. Large jars are also useful as their wide opening is easier to work with than a bottle with a smaller neck. If you intend to increase the amounts, buckets may be necessary for the 'seeping' process, for instance with the elderflower cordial.

Perhaps more important than the actual vessel though, is ensuring it has been sterilised properly. This will help your syrups and cordials keep for longer as it will remove any bacteria, yeasts or fungi and protect your liquids. The simplest way to sterilise your equipment at home is to wash the bottles or jars in very hot soapy water, rinse in more very hot water, and place them into an oven on the lowest setting (275°F/130°C/Gas 1) for twenty minutes. Ensure you use the vessels when they are still warm, and also that they are airtight when sealed to prevent bacteria entering the bottle. N.B: Do not put cold liquids into hot jars, or hot liquids into cold jars; this may result in the glass shattering; a messy and dangerous problem to fix!

W IS FOR...
WHITECURRANTS

Currants are another seasonal fruit which can be found in abundance during Autumn. If you find yourself with a glut of these delicious little fruits, why not try this simple recipe for white currant cordial? Do add more or less sugar than the recipe states (according to taste), depending on how ripe your currants are. If you are feeling particularly decadent, why not try adding a little of this lovely cordial to a glass of champagne?

White Currant Cordial

Ingredients

- 500g White Currants
- 250g Sugar
- 250ml Water
- Dash of Ginger
- Teaspoon of Orange Zest

Method

1. Place the berries, alongside the water in a large saucepan.
2. Cook over a low heat for a few minutes, then raise the heat and bring to a boil for two minutes.
3. Once the berries begin to burst, crush them against the sides of the pan with a fork.
4. Remove from the heat, and add the ginger and orange zest. Stir to combine. Cover the mixture and leave to stand for two hours.
5. Add the sugar and cook over a medium heat until the sugar is dissolved.
6. Strain the liquid through a muslin cloth. Your cordial is now ready to serve!

X IS FOR... XMAS

Christmas would simply not be Christmas without cinnamon. Cinnamon is a wonderfully evocative spice, and is found in many foodstuffs and beverages especially in winter and during the festive season. Its flavour is the result of an essential oil that makes up roughly 0.5 - 1% of its composition. This cordial is the perfect tipple to offer Christmas guests who would rather enjoy something alcohol-free, and is also delicious added to coffee or hot chocolate for a warming winter treat. You could also try it alongside some christmas cinnamon cookies.

Cinnamon Cordial

Ingredients

- 150g Bruised Cinnamon Sticks
- 200g Sugar
- 900ml Warm Water

Method

4. Place the ingredients into a sterilised jar and shake thoroughly. It is important at this stage to use warm water, instead of boiling water – otherwise the nuanced flavour of the cinnamon sticks will be lost.
5. Leave this mixture to stand for ten days, but return once a day to thoroughly shake the ingredients.
6. After the ten days are up, carefully filter the liquid through a clean muslin cloth, and into sterilised bottles to store.

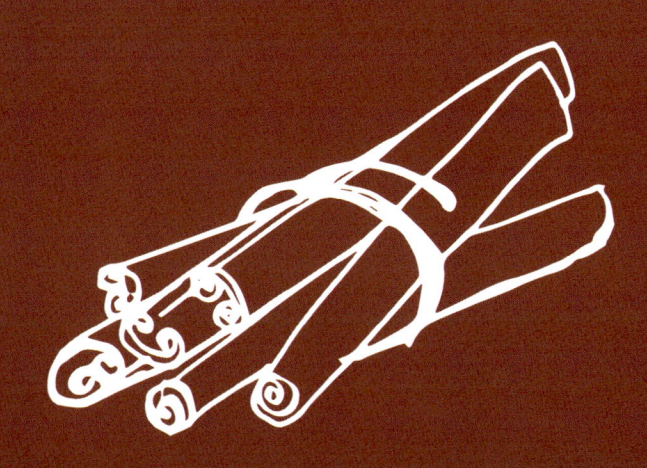

Y IS FOR... YULETIDE

Here is another festive recipe, this time using the rich, ruby-red fruit, cranberries. As cranberries can be quite tart and sour, especially when under ripe, do feel free to add more sugar to this syrup to taste. This will make a thoroughly refreshing beverage on its own, although why not experiment mixing it with the cinnamon cordial for a truly Christmassy taste? You could even add a little to your traditional cranberry sauce...

Cranberry Syrup

Ingredients

- 500g ripe Cranberries
- Boiling Water (to cover)
- 200g Sugar for every 200ml of juice produced.

Method

1. Place the fruit in a pan of boiling water and simmer gently for two hours. In order to keep the moisture in, place a slightly smaller pan lid over the fruit.
2. Strain the resulting liquid through a clean muslin cloth, measure carefully and add the sugar.
3. Bring to the boil again and skim off any scum which comes to the surface.
4. Leave to cool, and pour into sterilised bottles before storing.

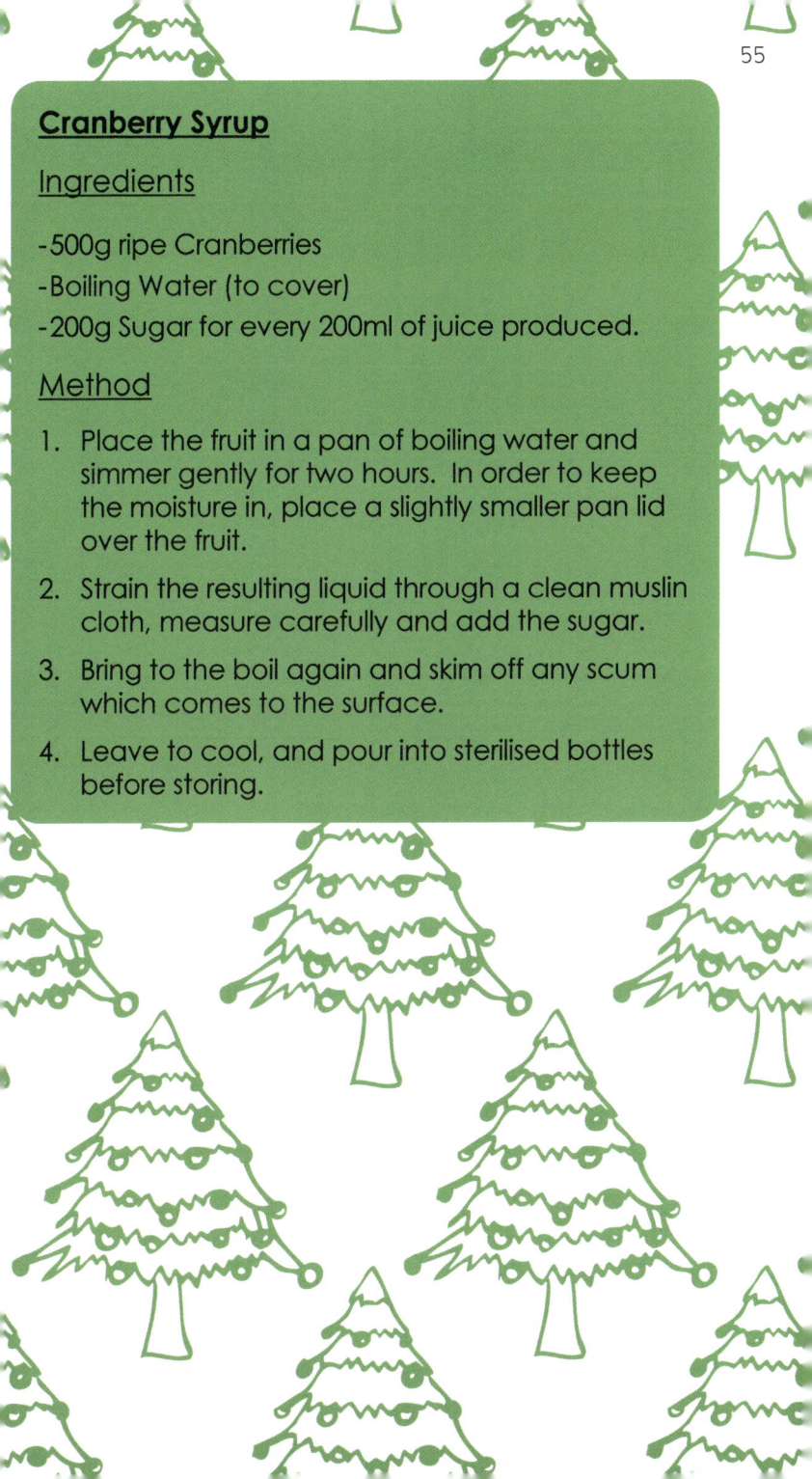

Z IS FOR... ZEST

Citrus fruits make wonderful-tasting syrups, and this one will also have the most gorgeous, vibrant colour thanks to the lemon's natural hue. This recipe for lemon syrup is a classic recipe to master. Once you have a supply of lemon syrup, you will amazed at how many uses you will find for it. Not only can it be diluted and enjoyed as a soft drink, but it is a really quick and easy way of adding an extra citrus tang to mixed cocktails at home. This recipe uses the juice, zest and rinds - really making the most of this wonderful fruit. Lemon syrup is also incredibly handy if you are making a lemon drizzle cake, or for that matter – any other lemon based dish (sweet or savoury).

Lemon Syrup

Ingredients

- 12 Lemons
- 500g Sugar
- 225ml Water

Method

1. Juice the lemons, but make sure to keep six of the rinds too.
2. Rub sugar onto the rinds of the six lemons and place into a large heavy-bottomed saucepan with the water.
3. Boil the mixture until clear, and then add all the strained lemon juice.
4. Simmer gently for five minutes.
5. Strain the mixture through a clean muslin cloth (optional).
6. Pour into sterilised bottles and seal. Garnish with curls of peeled lemon zest (optional!)
7. Store in the fridge or freezer, or use straight away.

TEN TOP TIPS

1. Get your utensils and equipment ready before starting.

2. Make time to make cordials regularly, so you always have a supply of ready-to-drink beverages stocked at home.

3. To prevent your cordials fermenting whilst they are in storage, stand the bottles in a saucepan of water on a thick pad of newspaper, with the water up to the necks of the bottles, and bring the water slowly to the boil and boil for five minutes.

4. Make sure you store your creations in sterilised bottles.

5. Sterilisation is easy, simply wash the bottles in very hot soapy water and place them into an oven on the lowest setting for twenty minutes.

ND TRICKS

6. Be sure to use your sterilised bottles while they are still warm.

7. Store your cordials in the fridge or freezer to lengthen their shelf life.

8. Experiment with mixing your cordials to make new variations.

9. Decant your cordials into pretty bottles with handwritten labels for a thoughtful gift.

10. Experiment with sugar free recipes for a healthy teeth-friendly cordial children will love. Always remember to taste as-you-go when adding sugar; as the natural tartness of the fruit will vary.

BUT MOST IMPORTANTLY, HAVE FUN!

Two Magpies

Copyright © 2013 Two Magpies Publishing

An imprint of Read Publishing Ltd
Home Farm, 44 Evesham Road, Cookhill, Alcester, Warwickshire, B49 5LJ

Commissioning Editor Rose Hewlett
Words by Amelia Carruthers
Design and Illustrations by Zoë Horn Haywood

This book is copyright and may not be reproduced or copied in any way without the express permission of the publisher in writing.

British Library Cataloguing-in-Publication Data. A catalogue record for this book is available from the British Library.

Printed in Great Britain
by Amazon